OPEN HEART

OPEN HEART

poems | Thomas Brush

LYNX HOUSE PRESS
Spokane, Washington

ACKNOWLEDGMENTS

Grateful acknowledgment is made to the following publications for poems, some in different form, that originally appeared in them.

Cimarron Review: "Saving the Orchard"
Dacotah Territory: "In a Classroom at Night"
Ellipsis: "Song"
Fine Madness: "In Celebration of a Friend's Birthday," "Saying Goodbye to the Graduates"
Mid-American Review: "Come Back," "Moon Landing," "Orcas Island," "Going Home"
Nimrod: "Last Summer," "Long Distance"
North American Review: "The State of the Art Sonnet"
Over The Wall Literary Review: "Welcome Home"
Poetry Northwest: "Exhibition Park," "Old Friends," "In the Badlands," "On Finding a Dead Swallow," "Transformations," "Night Skiing," "Artificial Heart," "The Side of the Road"
Quarterly West: "Another Soft Shoe for Spring," "Muse"
Sea Pen Press: "Golden Gate Park"
Seattle Review: "Closing Portland Meadows," "Cave Painting Above the Naches River," "Half-Way to Maury Island"
Shenandoah: "The Dreams of Gerard de Nerval"
Tar River Poetry: "Fog"

I would like to thank the National Endowment for the Arts, the National Endowment for the Humanities, the Washington State Arts Commission and Artist Trust whose support allowed me to complete many of these poems.

Cover Art by Megan Wolfe: *Wild at Heart,* oil on Panel, 18 x 24"
This and other artworks by Megan Wolfe can be viewed online at www.meganwolfeart.com.
Author Photo: Donna Herberger.
Book Design: Christine Holbert.

FIRST EDITION

Cataloging-in-Publication Data is available from the Library of Congress.

ISBN 978-0-89924-141-8

for Chris

CONTENTS

Do not be afraid. Why should my promises be vain? Jade and cinnamon: do you deny that such things exist? Why do you turn away? Is not my song a stream of balm? My arms are heaped with apples and ancient books; there is no harm in me; no. Stay. Praise me. Your praise of me is praise of yourself; wait. Listen. I will begin again.

—*John Updike*

"He had made his camp. He was settled. Nothing could touch him. It was a good place to camp. He was there, in the good place. He was in his home where he had made it."

—*Ernest Hemingway*

LOVE SONGS

They are reading while standing at bus stops,
Reading in the bath, on the couch, while walking
To work, while rain crosses the deserted streets. They are reading
On the wooden pews of churches, at the scarred tables
In second-hand stores, on buses, in limos, on benches
Outside the courthouse, in the Elm City
Diner; they are reading. Late at night, under the covers,
There are children reading by flashlight. There are children reciting
Poetry, standing in front of the class, in front
Of black boards crowded with the chalky remains
Of words. They are memorizing lines they will never forget.
They are reading holding on to the greasy straps
Of subways, in the warm comfort of libraries; they are reading
By moonlight, by candle light. They are reading
After dinner, by the fire with their feet propped up
On ottomans, in sidewalk cafés, in Paris, in pubs
While drinking beer.
                    And they are writing
On the floors of abandoned warehouses, writing on the sides
Of boxcars, in wet cement, carving their names in the trunks
Of cedars, eucalyptus, in groves of olive trees, in heartwood. They are
Writing on the damp walls of caves, in the airy wealth of penthouses,
In the sky, in the clouds. They are writing in the grass of parks, in the center
Of corn fields; they are writing with their bodies, on the breasts of men
And women, on their arms and legs, on their backs, on their thighs,
On the napes of their necks. They are trying out
Sentences, stanzas, chapters. They are mesmerized
By the shapes of letters, with the sounds
That leave and return as echoes. They are lost

In forests of chapters, in handmade paper, in used
Book stores, in mysteries, in grief, in tears.
They are walking through snowy fields of words.
They are sleeping between the dog-eared
Pages of books. They are dreaming.
They are in love.

OPEN HEART

The world is going down,
Again, or so the stories go
From every tweet and tabloid, from every politician
Up for grabs.
        But the pulsing neon signs in the windows
Of the Santa Fe Café still glow
On the freshly mown grass and dogs
Still romp through the wilderness
Of the park.
        Sure, sometimes at night I hear
My father coughing blood, asking for more
Time and there's never enough.
        There's good
In what he said, when he taught
Me how to tie a Blood Knot, standing in the cold waters
Of Gold Creek, the tippet may break
But never the knot, and in the words
He wrote, our lives as fragile and resonate
As the crystal hearts
Of the geodes he kept
On the mantle.
        Even now the flash of his smile
Looks up from a yearbook,
1935. Those strokes
Of luck as stubborn as the flowering
Dogwood fed by the ashes
Of the lost and what the wind and sky
Bring to anyone, anyone at all.

LUCK

Sometimes I'm lucky.
                    Some time
This morning, after six days, the rain stopped
And the grass applauded the sun.
                         Sometimes
Hummingbirds decorate the wild cherry trees, kaleidoscopes
Of wings whirling around the rotting fruit,
Vital as drops of blood. This afternoon I could feel
The summer heat as I water skied behind a Jeep
Down a narrow irrigation ditch
East of Yakima
                    decades ago.
          And last night, 1965, I heard them again,
Bob Dylan, Richie Havens and when we left
Smoking hand-rolled joints, singing
Down the sidewalks, Goldie shook
Her blonde curls with laughter.
                         Those times that keep me
Alive.
          Even now, when I pay my tab
And the waitress hands me my change, brushes her hair
Behind her ear, smiles, says she'll see me
Next time and will unless the moon
Washes the sea around me or the night
Dies of old age.
                    Luck,
Like these words that fall and leave
Their prints on the white world of the page,

Like the snow last winter that left
The ghosts of angels
Everywhere.

OCTOBER

October. A cold front
Coasting down from Canada, snow promised,
Tonight or tomorrow.
            The bed of the irrigation ditch
Is silver with ice, a ring-necked pheasant bursts
From a stand of saplings, quail bob away from me
Where just days ago we picked blackberries
And wild asparagus and listened
To her whisper, hush, *ssshh,* wait
For the moonlight to chase this month's monsters
Away, wait for the sound of cicadas, for coyotes
Howling down the day, wait for the deer standing by
The salt licks, and jack rabbits lining I-90
From Spokane to Coulee City, Woody Guthrie
Reclaiming the world
For all of us.
          So, I can spend my time
Here or back at the river, which is a kind of go-between,
Whose message is never the same. Or maybe I'm the go-between
From the present
To the past.
          So many things to remember, even the Ridgemont
Theater: Nights Of Cabiria, The Virgin
Spring, free cigarettes and coffee
During intermission. Jesus,
          I was young
And will be until darkness swallows
The sky and takes me
With it as it surely will.

It's a hot Saturday night and Johnny weighing in at 280 pounds is in the front row wallet chained to a back pocket left bicep reading Fuck Off right Jesus Loves You and I don't doubt either yelling Portia I love you Portia I am yours and I believe that too meanwhile the team is crouched in a surging ragged line in front of the Sin City Rollers swinging elbows knees swinging wide swinging wildly ducking beneath legs and arms shooting like heroin over the rail all the way to the stars and beyond the blockers and jammers the smallest fastest whipping past them all my god look at those satin shorts those fresh bruises blooming like night flowers sweating in the middle of a flat track hardwood jungle and suddenly I'm watching the round screen of a black and white 1950s t.v. Texaco Star Theater Your Show of Shows Imogene mugging for the camera Sid twirling a fake mustache leering at a showgirl who towers over him while Uncle Miltie slapsticks his way to center stage where Gorgeous George throws gold plated Georgie Pins to the raving ringside fans then gouges the eyes of the Masked Avenger slams his face into the steel turnbuckle tosses his platinum hair like a débutant until I can't stand up can't sit down as if somehow this was all that was left of the wild west side of America but then it all blurs to laughter and screams and I'm back in Vegas the Rat City Roller Girls gone after having been knocked out by The Fabulous Sockit Wenches and me drinking straight gin marking six numbers on a Keno card leaving Johnny at a 25 dollar blackjack table at Binion's with a four card 14 and the dealer showing 7 looking straight into her cleavage but thinking of those red satin shorts those tight red shorts saying Baby Baby hit me again!

WHEN I WAS A DUNCAN YOYO CHAMP

I could do anything. I could ride a skate board
Down the fairways of El Camino Real. I could stop trains
From sliding off the Bay Bridge. I could Shoot
The Moon with either hand. I could speak
In tongues. I could wear a blazing red windbreaker,
Carry a switchblade and a Zippo lighter, smoke
Luckies.
       When I was a Duncan YoYo Champ
I could ignore the rain filling the back streets
Of Oakland. I could Walk The Dog but I couldn't
Get past the snarling Dobermans straining in their chains
In Ezzard's backyard. I could strut
With the Banty Roosters, pick eggs
From the hens' nests before
They knew it.
       When I was a Duncan YoYo Champ
I rode with Marlon Brando astride his Triumph
Across the baked desert of middle California.
I sang Rock Around The Clock with Bill Haley
And The Comets. I performed
All the tricks; spun Around The World, Thread The Needle, Skin
The Cat, Rock The Baby. I put the yoyo
To sleep without saying
A word. But there's more.
       I won the prize one late afternoon on the black topped
Playground of Truman Elementary where, at recess,
While the other kids were bombarding
Each other with dodge balls or smashing tether balls or hanging
Upside down from the monkey bars

Like underage vampires, our insane,
Shell-shocked 5th Grade teacher instructed us
In close-order drill, screaming, "Your left! Your left!" then marched
Back to the classroom, muttering
"I don't know but I been told . . ." It seemed normal
At the time.

SO FAR, SO GOOD

> "And thanks be to God . . .
> that we lived so long and did so little harm."
>
> —*James Joyce*

The first day of summer I drove the road
To Stinson Beach, around the curves and switchbacks,
Scratched against the blue slate of the Pacific, where a single white cross
Pointed the way like the crosses that caress
The shoulders of the Italian Alps.
                    But then I was sliding
Down Chinook Pass, next to glacier
Fed streams—brook, brown, cutthroat—beaver dams that once held
Back the future, Roosevelt Elk, now protected, wading
The shallow ponds, and beyond, black bears sleeping
Through winter, where I once slept
Alone under the cover of guilt and regret, far away
From the damage of wars
That never stop, and the damage I did
In the swirl of what I can't even pretend was innocence.
                          Christ, this life
May be all we have but it will do,
Bleeding into the mystery
Of each day with grace and forgiveness, unfolding
Not as another hash mark
On a rock or tree or discarded calendar, but as a trailhead
To the approaching dusk
For all the good
It does.

ALL GOOD THINGS

The orange light that spills from the glowing Japanese lanterns
Hanging from the limbs of the willows, and the curves
Of the glass jars, reflecting the last light
Of day, covering the buds of pears to be brandy
Later, when we'll toast each other
And the coming year, and the what if
Of our lives.

Your hand written letters
In black ink, the graceful arcs
Of the js and ys, your signature
As steady as your voice once was,
Now gone. But this bundle lives forever
Tucked in the drawer of your desk and now in mine,
Which I read once a year on a day I pretend
Is your birthday. I don't know when
You died.

Owl feathers bunched like bouquets of flowers
On the back fence, stamped in browns and golds, never
Too late for the mail to come or the snow dreams that held you
As close as my arms. Counting the moments
As if they mattered, and the hope that will not
End.

Tossing stones into the pond we dug that summer, waiting
For the time when the circles come back
To us before we disappear. Little sleepwalker, why
Did you go so soon, and when will you return?

Dust, small wind, pools of sunlight
On the stone floor that can't be
Swept away. Good.
Good. Good.

IN THE DREAMTIME

"Aboriginal Creation myths tell of the legendary totemic beings who had wandered over the continent in the Dreamtime, singing out the name of everything that crossed their path . . . birds, animals, plants, rocks, waterholes—and so singing the world into existence."

—*Bruce Chatwin*

It doesn't get much better than that
But I can try, Lord, I can try. Words that create the world.
Swallows crossing the fields, searching
For insects, thigh high. Screech owls and Oregon Grape, snails,
Night crawlers, a limestone outcropping, the corpse
Of a nurse log buried in the wreckage
Of a rain forest. Palm trees in the Mojave Desert,
Aspens and alder growing through the front porch, Old Faithful
Spewing rainbows.
              So what if I'm an old man
Carrying a fistful of anger, my lungs scarred
With smoke, my eyes dim behind bifocals. My heart still
Works, beating the drum of what's next.
                      Take it from me
And Yogi . . . It ain't over . . .
And won't be until I can't lift
My head or feel the page under my arthritic fingers,
My tongue sticking out, my face
A Halloween mask.
                The world's still
Eden and it can be yours
For a song.

DREAM WARS

This morning mist rose from the valley,
The last hot day
Of July, strings the color of tarnished silver hanging
In the birch trees, wispy sheets floating like thoughts
I once had of something memorable, something
As transparent and important as that brief hour.
                              There's a stray
Cat, adrift in a pool of sunlight, and I envy
Him, King-Of-Sooner-
Or-Later, but not
                    now, winding my way
Through the smokeless air, so blue
It could be a lake turned upside down.
                              On the sidewalk
A rope of little kids holding hands swims by,
Led by a woman wearing a tee shirt emblazoned
With a baby hippo, and I begin
The morning ritual, sipping bourbon
Beneath Christmas lights framing the back
Bar, seeing the mirror as another body
Of water as holy as any, knowing how
I got here and why.
                    Two stools down
A man holds his beer in one fist, bleeding
From some dream war
All of us recognize and know
We can't win but we keep trying
One drink at a time.

THE DESATUEL RODEO

In April, 1967, my brother sent pictures
Of jungle clearings, of smoke filled villages, of helicopters rising
And falling, and of himself and Michael sprawled across sandbags, playing
Dead next to a gun emplacement
Just outside Pleiku. That's what I was thinking
About while I stood in the weak sunlight
In the back country of Okanogan County.

Sinlahekin Creek is banked with ice, and snow
Humps in the shade of lodge poles. Sap, the color of honey, beads
The fresh cut pine corral, where ponies, unshod and ragged as winter, kick,
Writhe, twist the rawhide halters, toss
Their uncut mane, toss the young
Indians who ride them bareback, as wild
As the wind across the valley which is the same
Wind that rides the broad black backs of water buffalo and crawls
Through waist high elephant
Grass.

Ten yards away a car catches
Fire and a laughing man dances
Away from the flames, throws a bottle
Into the windshield where it explodes in fragments
As silver as the streaks in his long hair.

No one, standing inside
That circle, turns from this place
Of worship, for that's what it is,
Called back every spring, dreaming of grasslands and rivers,
Of history as bright as those flares
Breaking over the lush, green hills.

Miles below, in the hard middle of August,
There will be a suicide
Race promoted by a local merchant. Horses and riders
Will fight to be first down the steep hill, then swim
Across the river and stagger through the spinning dust to the finish
Line, shining in the light that rises from the water and the light
Reflected from rice paddies a world away.

GAMBLING AT THE QUIL CEDA CASINO

> "These are the ones who escape
> after the last hurt is turned inward;
> they are the dangerous ones."
>
> —Joy Harjo, "She Had Some Horses"

Denise, the waitress, in a short black skirt and fishnet stockings,
Brings me coffee, and nearly in tears
Tells me her daughter's lungs are bleeding
Black mold, that she has to work
Double shifts, then hurries away when a man at the Black Jack table
Waves for more beer. Next to me a woman
Chain-smoking Pall Malls in front of a slot machine rubs
Her hands over the face of the screen, whispers to it
In a language I don't understand, as if it were her lover
And maybe it is, then collects
The paper chit that curls out of its chrome throat
Like a tongue.
           It's been twelve hours and I finally won
More than I lost but can never win
Enough. Outside it's nearly dawn. Stars
Shine through the haze like silver
Coins I could hold
In my hands if I could reach
High enough. But the creek is buried
Under asphalt, and there are no longhouses
But the one I just left and only the wind gallops
Toward the distant mountains.

ONE SONG

3 A.M., and I'm standing on the deck
Again, smoking another cigarette, looking out
Through the rain, where just a few hours
Ago lightning burned its jagged signature
Through the foothills, wondering when the moon
Went to sleep, when September will stretch
Its long legs.
      When will what I've written
Become true? For the story of a life
Lingers like the crows
Looking down from the power
Lines or the fireflies flashing
In the deep bed of the garden.
      What then? Nothing really, just the not forgetting
That provides the tattered remains
Of an overcoat to keep me
Warm until morning, a realization
That the singing
Never stops.

NURSE

We've all heard the old joke
When someone at the next table calls
The waitress "nurse," and we smile or look
Away, consider the gin, take another drink. Or the one
    about the man
Leaving the bar, walking out into sunlight that staggers
Him down the steps, who imagines, before he starts
His car, that the road home is not his road, is not straight,
But curves like the horizon in the rear-view mirror,
    that the steep hills
Belong in Colorado or Montana, that the drinks have worked
And he's happy being lost.
                          Still, we know "nurse"
Is not a bad joke, that the blood in plastic
Sacks suspended above us is real and no worse
Than the cheap vodka the end of the month forces on us,
    or the cold change
Of seasons that snaps us awake when we find ourselves
In a strange town, miles from home, working
Through the third Scotch over, knowing taste
Depends on who we are and not where. At that moment
We want no explanation, only the bite of smoke, the solid wood
Of the bar, and the lovely question on the waitress's face.

LISTEN

Nothing's going on tonight, unless
You count the spiders
Walking down the wooden slats of the balcony or the smell
Of cooked cabbage in the hallway, or the old man
In 307, coughing and smoking
Chesterfields, reading mysteries, sometimes
Reliving the jungles that took
His boyhood, and the year that took
His daughter who left long ago and will never be
Back.
      A cat howls on the back stairs,
And the free movie shown on a brick
Wall of the tavern next door is Cool Hand Luke.
      It's last call for the sun
Sinking into nothingness,
For now. Or forever. Who knows?
Not me.
      But I can pretend
The air is heating up, that the clouds are billowing
Above the rolling deck, above the frost
Covered bow, above the waves, the sea and what's left
Of Deception Pass, and listen
To what saves me, Paul Newman singing "I don't care
if it rains or freezes . . ." just a line
Thrown toward the dock or written
By the lights that go out
One by one.

SAVING THE ORCHARD

This afternoon I started again. Drinking
The bitter tea I love. Lifting weights in short, hard three minute
Bursts until I'm out of breath and have to stop. I finished reading
A novel about a man who slowly forgot everything,
As if time had stumbled and he was lost in a storm of soft,
Gray noise and nothing more.
                              But I remember the orchard,
Smudge pots burning against the frost, a hundred dark fires
Warming the hard, green buds, spider webs glistening, gleaming
Like black stars in the corners of the windows, my mouth and nose
Oily with soot, as if I could return and relive everything. As if it really
Happened. And it's 1959, our lives falling
Through the years as fragile as our faith
In those small flames.

MUSE

Tonight I'm through with the old deaths, fathers
I could never call by name, words
Taken from the *Book Of The Lost:* the back streets
Of Tacoma, L.A., the sweet taste of the bottle, the battles
The rust won. Tonight I'm finished
With the old man curled in his own
Tears, his mind spilling over
Into the drunken dreams that hold him
Up. I'm going to forget the faces
That wander the frozen halls of every hotel
That ever called, the sagging beds of flesh, wherever the nameless
Gather around me.
                   Tonight I won't sleep
It off, but cover my son when he kicks the blankets
To the floor, and watch the sky lighten, as it must, toward morning,
And wait for the music to fall from the trees, then the sun
To wake the drowsing grass and the cat that sleeps
Each night on my car, whose muddy paws
Leave tracks across the canvas roof that I'll ride under
All the way to work and back
To love and the home that tells us both
That we're alive and mean
To stay that way.

NIGHT SKIING

Rising,
The old-fashioned wooden lifts float
Through the broken blue halos, cross shadows
With the empty chairs coming down
Through the falling snow,
Heavy and thick as the sky
Will be when morning sweeps the clouds
From the distant corners of the stars.
                    But for now it's the slow ride
Above the shining clouds of cedars—
Bone-dust, quick lime—that I don't want
To end, already imagining the view
From the summit, the black mountains and the long curve of the world,
The last, late run along the frozen lake
Where ice still scrapes the sheer sides of the cliffs,
Then the warm waters of the distant river, even the earth
That by now could be miles away. And when the lifts pause
At the edge of motion, I dream
That death is like this, a quiet
Net of sleep with nothing to do
But lean back and not wake,
Simply love the moment
Just below the surface of the air
I tread, that holds me and will not let go,
Not here, not yet.

COME BACK

In some narrow hallway of a year choked with flames
You cross the fields toward home, wade the ruts of mud
And rust, count the hours the rain gave back. You run
A hand over a face you cannot see, remember
A car that shuddered, then broke
Through the ice of the river
And disappeared. You hold a rag to the place
Where pain has eaten a hole in your throat, hold
A fistful of coins so close
They burn.

> In April, so long ago, there was salt on the table, a closet
> of leaves, your wife ironing, folding the comfort
> of clean, soft clothes. But you saw death
> as a mountain falling through the sky, and you rose
> in darkness, kissed the dream of her face and ran
> into the only life that ever mattered.
>   Now the world is the slurred mouth
> of dust, the cold doors of the river that never close, the woman
> next to you, drunk and in tears.

Well, there's nothing I can do with spring
Freshly risen from the floor of longing, and the old rituals
Still spilling from your lips, except to say I'm sorry
For us all and wish you back,
As if I could climb some ladder
Of air toward the one small leaf
The twilight left, toward the broken fingers
Of the stars, toward the last hotel burning toward morning
And the only words I have
For love.

"Can't repeat the past? . . . Why of course you can."

—*F. Scott Fitzgerald*

Just flashes,
Returning like the distance
From every house I've ever lived in.
   Two split bamboo fly rods nearly a hundred
Years old hanging from wooden pegs fitted into the clear pine
Walls of the cabin. A Royal Coachman skating down a riffle
Of Manashtash creek. My Grandfather's
Medical books we read as kids, horrified
By the black and white pictures
Of diseases we couldn't imagine.
    The brass rail on Sunday
Afternoons at Murphy's Pub, Gatsby decking out his dream
". . . With every bright feather that drifted his way." And my father
Choking on a piece of bacon in the psychiatric ward in Western State
And his brother who put a gun to his head in Bolinas, California,
Two weeks later.
    That night I tried to write about them
By the light of a Coleman lantern, the mantel as fragile
As burning wings or the words I couldn't find.
    And that's all right. For now there are no lights
That I can see, the sky clear. It's the silence I long for,
And emptiness, just marks on an envelope like aspen leaves
Floating on the river of the past.

THIS TIME

"The medical profession may save your life,
but it can never make your life worth saving."

—*James Dickey*

The moon's shattered skull wobbling
On the mirror of the lake. The slow walk
To the wet edge of the shore
Where I take in the warm night
Air and the frogs' soft hoots
That are peaceful and comforting
As if cruelty had disappeared,
And there are no lies
To trumpet or bow down
To, nothing could be bought
That would do any good.
                        There's a rose
Bush in full bloom next to the bar where I drink in
The afternoons, Neil Young shooting
His baby, two waitresses studying the Racing Form, a couple
In the dart pit playing 301.
                        What is it,
This time? Only the moments
Inside or out, someone lying
Beside me, her hands pushing the storm
Away, maybe the circles of shade
Beneath the apple trees, horses
Galloping over the dunes to the ocean.

Just a few words,
Laughter, friendship, perhaps
Love, the only provisions
That mean anything
In this sweet life
That only happens
Once.

TIME TO GO

Time to go.
Almost. Sunlight beginning
To cross the street like a man on his way home
At the end of the night shift. A few stragglers huddle
Near the bus stop, look
Up as the light approaches, but don't move.
          Maybe I should take a walk,
Down the hill, along the edge of the park
Where two starlings gaze down from the highest branch
Of a maple tree, to Greenlake where joggers and skaters
Slide past me making their daily circuits, where a single cormorant
Eyes me warily, and black and yellow striped
Turtles line up on a half-submerged log,
Basking in the light flashing up
From the water. Watch the buffleheads
Dive and come up with small silver fish, watch the old men
Sitting in lawn chairs, fishing poles in forked sticks
Beside them, half-asleep, half-awake
In Spring's gratitude.
          Could there be time enough for that? Stretched
Out on a wooden bench, waiting for dusk, until the moon shows
Itself, a witch's moon, blue, its face pocked with silver scars
I can wish on?
          There's plenty of time to walk back. Time
For the god of sky and water
To take another turn. God of here
And now. God of wisdom,
Who knows the world's time
Is time enough.

ON FINDING A DEAD SWALLOW

Having fallen this far
Through the wet branches and tangled webs of light,
Into the crumbling remains
Of twigs and the sunken nests
Of last week's snow, you can no longer move
Your wings now soaked and stuck together
Like the rain and lightning
That have been falling
All morning long.
                Here the first warmth
Of noon holds us together, the bright wind, and the last
Comfort of each small fire, feather and eye,
Turned toward my rising breath
And all that's left of yours,
Still pulled by the ancient gravity
Of the long dead
Stars and all the cold heavens
They shine through.

THE ZOO KEEPER'S PROMISE

Finally! And why not? Why not
Have hippos splashing under the back yard
Sprinklers, alligators swaying down the aisles
Of the nearest supermarket. Why can't tapirs
Direct traffic outside the sushi palace, and let oxen carry
Only the heavy burden of themselves. Let wart hogs
Root through the rhododendrons and dine
On old roses. Why shouldn't the sloths be shaken
From their lethargy and smile at us
From the eucalyptus trees, perhaps a giraffe
Would stick his tongue through the open bedroom
Window, and power poles could be draped with the colorful banners
Of pythons. Let's have hyenas laugh
With the drunks staggering across the crooked sidewalks,
And bears ride bicycles
To the mayor's house, while overhead
All the birds of the world
Sing their familiar songs, and we, not dressed
In leather and furs, could at last,
Be open, free and naked
As the day we were born.

TRANSFORMATIONS

I can't remember when they began,
The changes. The old Plymouth
At the curb is the sea lion
I shaped from clay when I was a senior
In high school, the only decent work
I made in that forgettable class. The white towel
On the neighbor's line is a snowy owl
Shorn from some sea
Of ice and salt. A poem
Is painted across the hot sky
In gleaming Disney
Colors—smog, ice, the shadows
Of dawn. All changed
In a cavern of signs and spells, echoes
Floating on the fallen tides of mud and honey,
Ink smeared across the wet fields
Of notebooks, ink blurred
To nothing recognizable.
                    But there were islands
Of cottonwoods drifting in lakes of wheat, the white tufts
Caught on fences and the rippling backs
Of cattle swimming in the shallows
Of shade. And my friend,
The lawyer, who took me in that last year
When nearly everyone had given up
On me. He told me any fool can graduate
And I proved him right. He created
In me the possibility of something
Better than those days pruning hops

In the hard winds of Moxee, Sunnyside,
Those long nights sweating atop a jitney, stacking
Wooden pallets decades high, when the only thing that counted
Was the dreaming
Not of loss but what I could find
In the promise of my own hands.

MOON LANDING

Moon. Just above the worn crest
Of willows or grass or history. Moon
That made the future livable, that lit up
The small room of wonder, that came out
Of hiding from behind the heavy slab of the sky.

    But they came home riding the fog that flooded the back roads
    of Kansas, walking down the ruins of a smile, drowning
    in the soft soil of some imagined Midwest, or cold and coming to
    in some distant corner of the world you never saw.

The wooden floor turning in the one blue circle
Moon made.

    Not a gray field of dust and ashes, the leftovers
    of the rich, green flames, the blackened
    metal, the face of the sun torn and bursting.

Just once more.

Moon was the mother of laughter, not the old
Woman lying down in loneliness, holding her head in her hands,
Crying for what she is. Not moon our fathers see
In the shallows of their breath,
Drunk and destroyed by grief, and failure
Of what they thought
Was nerve.

                    But moon
Rising from a lake years ago, where she leaned
Down to them in that glory
That should never die.

        If there was a way out
        If there was a boat made of water
        If the air wasn't bruised
        with blood

If there was moon
        we would smile and never wake

        Moon
        landing without a splash
        or a ripple
        in the dead arms held out to us
        like this

COUNTING THE HOURS

I could count the days on Phinney Ridge by the way
Mist walks up from the lake, or the way leaves
Fill the streets after rain.
                    The remains of fallen
Plums bruising the deep grass, a path
Through a graveyard, freshly cut flowers etched
Against the chiseled stones, elms
Rigid as guards at the edge of covered lanes, hours
Of prayer, of anger, of refuge,
Of forgiveness.

                Hours from home spent
In countries whose language I don't speak, newspapers
Of no use, borders I continue to cross, listening
To the beauty of songs, praying for the reflected beauty of stained glass
That needs no interpreter. The ruins
Of churches, a tarot of voices, a column
Of lost friends I see nightly. The glory of the unalterable,
Unassailable, insistent
As the heart's sure voyage.

                And later, the afternoon
Breeze tapering off like the tide receding
Over the worn stones off Deception Pass.
I used to walk the trails there, with an arm
Of driftwood for a walking stick, along the curving track
Of the Great Northern where once we put pennies
To be flattened into sacred tokens
We hoarded like love.

Hours counting scraps
Of poems I meant to write, names of places
That return as simply as breath: White Swan, Sawmill Flats,
La Paz, Berlin, Paris.

They say I should write
What I know, which isn't much, the two
Of us on the quiet beach, time to drink
And laugh, to plant the garden, to read, to remember
The day the Duwamish River disappeared, the decaying
Cities holding their own, a wreath of human
Ears, the remains
Of life, a lost and found
For the dead.

NAMING THE DAYS

It's been awhile since I've given
Much thought to distance, to the past.
You know,
                looking over my shoulder
At what I thought happened, but this morning
It's easy considering the false
Dawn and clouds so dark they seal
The sky that it could be night
All day long.
              I might have to consult
A calendar, if I have one, wipe the dates off the windows,
See what the traffic is like. Watch the horses
Pull the milk truck to market, the reins like a dirty
Necklace, but it doesn't make much difference.
              I'll think of something, a hawk's wing
Sewing the mountains together, moss draped
Over the roof of a barn, some faraway meadow
Or another. It might be Independence Day or Easter, maybe
All Saints Day, or a day cut with sunlight
Falling through the screen of weeping
Willows, grass under my bare feet.
              What I want is the wind
Blowing the curtains, until I wake
To the freckled map of your breasts,
To your face lost in sleep
But not lost
For long.

CANNON BEACH

Today there's too much heat. The sun
Is a bowl of honey, creamy, thick, sweet as the sting of sugar
Clicking in its cells. My brother wades waist deep
In the heavy waves as they sink
Haystack Rock, then slide
Over the flashing whips
Of seaweed.
         The shells are scraps of fire
And every piece of driftwood charred bone. There is no wind
To walk. Every kite,
Trailing tendrils of salt, lies still,
Silent as the broken circle of a sand dollar.
In two nights there will be lightning, flames
Entering the cold whispers of the ice house, quiet
As the dead now dressed
In sawdust and ashes, who wake and descend
The molten rocks, searching the tide pools
For movement, but all the fish are belly up, crabs out of sight,
Starfish welded to the walls of the blazing cave.
         He can't speak
Of summer, his war
Is still shimmering on the back of the stove,
Blood soup we can't get
Enough of, the pictures of Saigon
Scarring his face like those photos of Japanese soldiers
In the tabloid still holding on
To their names in some island jungle, forty years too late
For anyone, rifles clean and oiled, bayonets free
Of rust, still lethal as their promise.

When he was sent to Hawaii
For R&R he didn't visit the ancient wreckage
Of the Arizona nor walk the imported beach.
He spent the hoarded days of rest drunk
And in bed with a girl whose hair was long and black as sleep.
Even here,
The lunatic storm blows
The future away, our eyes fall
To coals, the grassfire walks its erratic steps
Across the nearest border, as if the corpse
Of a saint or an angel rose on blistered feet,
Trailing tears and the bloody flowers of ecstasy.

BLACK OUT

"I heard the news today, oh boy . . ."

—*Lennon/McCartney*

The cedars noisy
With birds, the slow turn of the sea, snow geese flying
Home. But not us. We pulled up
Stakes and went elsewhere. We won't return.

Thunderstorms gather miles
Off the Atlantic
Coast. The afternoon sky begins
To melt, no snow on Kilimanjaro. The story
Once told is now soft rain
Blowing through the pages of the dead.
We died from indifference, unbowed
To the power of anything
But money.

      Half a country away a C–17 comes
To a full stop, the flag draped coffins hidden
From view. What do we want? Why
The secrets, the lies, while they lie
Out of sight? So much is redacted, blacked out,
Their names, at least for now, and the names of cities and towns,
Villages, dates we might remember, rivers, roads
We might recognize. Why is that?
      These aren't hard
Questions. The answers are
Easy. If anyone asks, but no one does.

LONG DISTANCE

You call, late, when you can't sleep or drink
Enough so it doesn't matter. Mostly
You're funny, tell impossible stories
Of gambling with Howard Hughes at the MGM Grand, of the blood
Rites of a teen-aged gang in a California city
That never existed, or the parade of girls
Who shared your bed. Stories
That are better than what happens
To either of us.

        But last night the past stood
Howling, and we were back in San Francisco
Before Tet, before we died, drunk as the cold
Stones of the Tenderloin, waiting for the bars
To open. We hid with the pigeons
On the sawdust floors. The Scotch we drank tasted better
Than anything we ate that week. The sidewalks ran
All the way to the wharf where we waded a dream
So deep we couldn't get lost
No matter how we tried.

        Now, in Austin, Vice President
Of an insurance company, wise as Stevens himself, you manage
To keep all of your balances, say the wolves can't get past
The outskirts of town, and smile.

And yet, we call back those strung out
Voices on the lines that hold us
Together, as if our days were still
A hillside street we could cross, dodging parking meters
And screeching cars, the shouts of all those strangers
So much like us we could cry.

HALF-WAY TO MAURY ISLAND

Thank God for the rain,
For the green home of moss and mud
And for the old wooden hull of the steam ferry
San Mateo that still floats
From Tacoma to Tahlequah,
And for all the rusting steel decks and rotting
Dugouts and the single mountain that holds
Puget Sound in place, and for the salmon that rise
Like the lost language of the Salish and for the clean
Hands of the rivers and the wet and swollen stones
That balance the earth beneath us.
      And thank the damp breath
Of the leaves, and the sweet torrent
Of twigs stirring the black bark, and the branches
That twist and swell in the writhing
Trail of air, and the long, secret whistle of geese
That crosses that falling sky, and the sobbing music
Of the tides, and for what I can take
From this sinking island and call it
Home.

The clouds come down all the way
From the Strait of Juan de Fuca. They say it's the rip-tide
That makes them drift so. They say it's their place
To hide. The stains on the wooden floor are cold and slant
Toward the muddy road, the blue fields, and yellow
Grass, toward the ghost horses standing, asleep,
In the lost pasture. We hide in what we were,
Old letters in a stone jar, summer
Crouching in the attic, the promises we meant
To keep. And in the darkness time is safe
And quiet, and we hold it between us
Like a sleeping child.

WHAT I CARRY

"You smoke too much, drink too much and write too much."

—*Observation by an acquaintance*

I sit in the sunlight on the back deck
Of Murphy's Pub, light another Marlboro, sip
A Tequila Madras, consider the beautiful
Waitress as she sways
From table to table, then write
In the small notebook
I carry with me, always.

CANYON DE CHELLY

It was what we came for, the heat
And the pictures drawn on the canyon
Walls. The pink and gold stripes writing down the ruins
Of the past. A meandering stain of green
Water, where a dragonfly's iridescence
Hovers over the scattered reeds, the deep hoots
Of a frog, boulders the size of cathedrals, towers
Of sandstone and silica. Dry heat, not even
A scar on the hardpan. So much is gone
But not everything.
       It's been nearly a century
Of stories, some are mine, just songs
Sung, a handful of wishes and some come true.
       Maybe we've taken a wrong turn
But the small brown and gray sparrows balanced
On cactus spines don't seem to think so. Above the plain
Glistening with mica, the silence of an owl
Soars through the darkness, then dust devils
Gathering wind, small funnels of rage,
Coming our way.
       Maybe the sparks from the clay
Mouth of a chiminea can save us. Those fragments
That mirror age and never let go.
       Remember childhood,
The afternoon of the concert, all hope and light, Joan Baez
In Newport, 1959, "Hush little baby, don't you cry . . ."
A lifetime disappearing. No resurrection
For me, at least not now, and now the night sky
Is so dark that all we can see or want
Is that distant field
Of stars.

BEFORE I FORGET

I want to tell you
About the girl in front of me
At the drug store, the red and yellow sunburst
Tattoo burning her neck as if the sun
Had set there and she never wanted it
To leave. That Tim can identify most birds
By their calls, while I can barely see
Them, my eyesight diminishing
As I age. That I sometimes feel
Like a man caught in a flood
Of starlight drifting through what passes
For rain.
       Or how snow melt once colored
The stones in the bed
Of Rattlesnake Creek.
       I want to tell you what it's like
To listen as the last of the music
Escapes the nearby bar, lingering
Like names I once knew, maps
Of places I'd traveled, rooms
I've lived in.
       And Rebekah's red hair, curled
Around the light spilling from the bedroom
Window, one of the things I want
To remember.

AFTER

Some day, after all
This is gone, before night settles
Its final argument, you may find yourself
Sitting on a stone wall, built before the Civil War,
In the quiet vista of North Carolina, the freckled dawn
Bathing your legs, the wind hardly moving,
You might think of Yeats' poem "Brown Penny," I once sent
To you, and maybe you'll smile at that
Memory and what we had, when you had
The wings of a girl, and when the gold coin
Of the moon looks down
On you you'll know (and I certainly don't
Have to tell you) where to find the green bank
Where we crossed the river and watched
Deer dozing in the late afternoon
Shade, and when rain opens its wings in the forgiving
September heat, to drench the willows and live oaks, the coots diving
For their lives, the songs you can still hear
Trailing through the ripening grass, everything, you'll take off
Your wet clothes and wade through the silver air,
And say nothing as the warm blue world takes you
In its arms.

IF I WROTE FOR A THOUSAND YEARS

A single white cloud
Caught in the hedge that borders
The back yard. Two mourning
Doves guarding the fence
As if it would keep them
Alive. A note from a former student asking
For help pinned in the dust of the cork board,
Another voice saying
Goodbye. Gravel paths that lead to the cottonwoods
Where the homeless curl
Under a starlit sky.
      If I wrote
For a thousand years I couldn't find the words
To describe the beauty the tribes
Died for, their language in ruins, the syllables
Only shards of meaning that can't help
Anyone or stop the snow melt draining
From some lost lake, but if I continue
They'll be there waiting
To take me with them.
      Just like the movie that ends
Well, but I don't know how
This will end, how easy and how hard
It is to hold and then let go,
Knowing love is worth the telling
And all that's left.

BLESSINGS

There are songs that return
As surely as dawn, drumming across the damp earth,
Cast back like the rushing waters, here and there along the stream beds
We used to wade, the lyrics as permanent as the tattoos
We bled into our arms years later, or the dirt roads
We walked that don't exist
Anymore.
         As now, one shot of cortisone eases the song
Of pain that never goes completely away, and maybe it will help me
Sleep and forget the dreams where I spend decades retaking
Tests on subjects I never studied, classes I never took,
Failures that never leave.
         But there are songs
Wrapped in the lightness of time,
When I again kiss the lips of a 16 year old girl.
        And there are times when I wake, knowing
It's not simply age I can't stop, nor the twilight
In flames outside the windows, the oil
Strewn fields, bomb fragments still exploding,
The children not safe
Anywhere,
       the grotesque faces
Grinning for more guns,
         and I take down
The book of poems, re-read the beauty of James Wright,
Light another cigarette, run my fingers
Over the future, tilt my head to the bird calls
That make the day
Bearable, stretch the sad muscles of my left shoulder for Nicole

Who spreads lotion, kneads with the warmth
And pressure of her hands, that lifts the weight
Of the present until the music is all
That matters.

ANITA O'DAY

Someone's singing somewhere
Beyond the mist of the park, a voice that makes me think
The poem is almost finished, these days
Having forgotten so much, having to look up
The simplest words, trying to understand
The emptiness. Duane, being treated
For lymphoma, jokes
About it and late last night, watching "Jazz on a Summer's
Day," I'm back with her in a bar in Pioneer Square listening
To her sing "My Funny Valentine"
So beautifully that I can't
Disappear.

CAVE PAINTING ABOVE THE NACHES RIVER

I wonder what he thought
Walking back through the sagebrush and sumac, the goldenrod
Like gathered heat around his waist, through the last glare
Rising from the river? And later, when he uncovered the shadow-
Filled cave and felt the cool granite
Walls, blank as creation, under his hands?
                              Whether he was moved from centuries
Of tradition or found his own, there was someone's heart
Pumping in every bent leg that crosses the ceiling, every claw
That strikes sparks, every splinter
Of bone and broken antler
That still calls. I see him
Standing by firelight, tracing teeth
And hoofs and curving flesh with blackened fingers,
Then mixing the thick resin
Of berries and pinesap, the crushed flames of clay
That marked their flight, finally drawing
The red line of imagination
From the eyes of antelope and black bear
Straight down,
Past the falling shale and coming history
Of loss, to the washed-out sides and purple hooked jaws
Of the dying salmon
Going back to the gravel nests
Where they began and begin
Again, where each stroke
Whether tail or hand or breath of God
Is the gesture we recognize
And live.

LAST SUMMER

It was what we searched for
Under a sky bright enough to believe
In gifts, when we crossed the broken ribs of the corduroy road
That led to the ruins of Copper City, and walked the clear shallows
Of the Bumping River, watching the lowered heads
Of sheep graze on what was left of autumn. And again we counted
The circles made by the small flat stones we skipped
Across the water, when we were sure enough, lying
Half-asleep after swimming, to let silence be the present
We could keep. The days were filled with the widening
Surface of sunlight, moonlight, the deepening pools
Of the afternoons, or the mayflies
Rising like jewels through the heat.

      As now, twenty years
Removed, I still feel those warm nights
On the river, fishing illegally by the flame
Of an old lantern, and the fruit bats
Coming down like moving holes in the darkness
To brush the light then disappear, and the beauty
Of distance that stands behind every word
I ever wrote, every letter, every sunken step
Of grass that still calls.

      My God, I wish those shimmering days
Back, when we knew who we were, and the fever
Of morning that walked with us down the wet path
Home, the gunny sack soaked silver with Dolly Varden,
Your son asleep on the screened porch, and your laughter
Waking him, and your face
Close enough to touch.

FOG

Fog, heavy and thick
As smoke, rises from the warm bowl of the lake
As it rose around you when you sank
Into the rising stream of winter. I remember you waving
From a window near the back of the plane, your small blurred face,
And the dull lights of the runway, the rain
That began as thunder, and the gray clouds
Falling all the way to the infield. Fog
That melted the dark edge of the road, that erased the mountains,
The trees, and their brother the snow, the growing sky.
Fog that whispers with your voice this morning, that walks
Around me as dew in the deepening grass. On a day
Like this. On a day that can't seem to start
Without you, but floats in a dull grayness, pain,
Such as the lost whalers must have felt
When they at last broke out into the calm
Of an empty sea, as the ground must have been
As it came up and you fell into it
Forever.

ON THE AURORA BRIDGE

For a moment nothing moved
But the rain smearing the stoplight
A half-block away and the hanging
Baskets swaying against the lampposts
That lined the Montlake Cut,
When a woman leaned over the railing.
                                    I don't know
What happened, had she merely paused
On her morning walk, fascinated
By the luminescent wakes
Crisscrossing the cold
Water so far below or was she so depressed
By whatever life she led that she let herself fall
Into the forgiving air?
                          Since so much of my life
Now is imaginary, I can see her
Arm in arm with a lover, mother, child
Walking back through the damp streets,
Under the thick leaves of every tree
She passed, drinking the hot tea she left
Steeping in a ceramic pot on the kitchen table, home
And the comfort of place, delight
In the hours she'll pass until sleep.
                          Maybe patience is simply recognizing
What's possible. Maybe you saw her. Maybe
She reading this now.

WOODLAND PARK

It's quiet now, early morning and the little kid
Walking up the slide
The wrong way and falling back, then trying again
As well he should, isn't talking. But the animals
In the nearby zoo are waking up, their cries a menagerie
Of welcome guests. Now the birds, a Cooper's Hawk threatening
The sparrows and blue jays,
Begin the conversation. Saying, maybe
We can change the lyrics
The leaves wrote, forget
The icy side of the sky, even though it's too late to help
The man who couldn't rise from the grave
Of the doorway or the girl who took my hand
And never let go.
       I remember lying
On the cooling sands on the shore of the American River,
Watching a shower of shooting stars
Cross the midnight sky and the granite rock we dove
From in the heat of the afternoons, a cabin
At the edge of a bluff, a tin of bacon grease
Next to the wood stove, trout frying in a cast iron skillet,
Onions and garlic. The fullness of the days
To come.
       So, I'll take what I'm given and accept
The inevitable, walk the growing fields
Of the park, smiling, happy.

GOING HOME

Here is the stain of the heart's first blood
Here is the song of breath
Here is the darkness that melts the earth
Here is the sleep of your tongue

The weeks of warmth filled the air with hope, the long
White waves washing the morning around you, the clutter of books
That said, Quiet, a porcelain doll nodding its answer. There was
          your mother
Stirring the kitchen again. Then silence. Going home.

                        There was a train
Riding thirty feet of air, and the house shook with steam
And the whistle. There was the winter night when fire took half
The town. Even now there is someone calling your name.

                       How we are still
Children, how the past never ends. The cough of an engine
Or a sky streaked with smoke brings news fifty years old, prayer
And a rosary, a single candle that turns the river to flames.

It was the one planet that rose from the sea.
It was the floating bloom of air.

                       How easy
It is to remember. How easy to imagine morning
For the first time.

WELCOME HOME

January. And I'm sick
Of despair, dogs in the kitchen, drunks in the attic,
Food on the table
          and no one in sight.

    I want to kick up my heels on the dusty floor
Of the moon, skate across The Sea of Tranquility, find a wide path
Of weightlessness where I can drift all the way back
To innocence. I want to say something

Worthwhile. I want to be in the photograph of the blue curve
Of an earthrise, sit on the shoulder of a red dwarf,
Assist in the birth of a nova. I want to swallow the rising tongues
That never stop. I want to believe everything
Is all right.

        Some days I'm lucky
And the woods walk up to my door. I find a cave
Veined with warm fissures of myth and the roots of pines
That eat them. Some days the dry shadows of the sun paint their animals
On rock walls, songs of the earth, songs of the sky,
While I watch, still listening,
Still wishing I could change
This frost burnt beginning of any year.

IN CELEBRATION OF A FRIEND'S BIRTHDAY

Outside, the rain is starting
Again, small fires on Yesler, the red smoke
Of neon, the broken amber of shattered glass, shallow pools
Of oil, but I'm thinking of other celebrations,
Of the woman who walks daily from alley to alley calling
Cats as if they were her children, the bulging sack
At her waist as tribute to the choices
She makes out of morning, out of loneliness.
                         We have such choices
Gathering what we think
We need, the leaning shadows of friends, there,
Against the peeling wall, or someone's face
Dripping through the faded silver of a mirror. Celebrate. Make the day
More than it is, as if we can repeat
The past. And if we can, then I want them back—
The Athenian, The Merchant's Café
The way they were yesterday, years ago,
The crab fresh, the coffee steaming, Kleven standing
At the bar, toasting everyone who comes in
And meaning it, Hugo at a window
Seat writing to Blessing. Celebrate
The moment. Let the past be
Born again, pressed between pages
Of grief and gratitude and let the future
Be.

MILROY PARK

There is the stone table—
Uncles in shirtsleeves playing
Checkers, taking turns sipping
Bourbon from a pint bottle
That is always in one pocket
Or another—I could cover
With one of time's calloused hands.

And there the old women
Talking of operations, grandchildren, tired
Husbands, talk the day
Away, moving only to keep up
With the constant movement of the sun
Or with grandchildren risen from the grass
With skinned knees or pleading

For ice-cream. But today it's replaced
By a mall where the only sounds
Are from sales reps, and the music
From hidden speakers or the absurd ring
Tones of cell phones. Here no one talks
To strangers or whispers
Dirty jokes or listens
As gossip opens the gates
To the cobbled lanes of poetry.

GOLDEN GATE PARK

From the crowded track of the freeway
The horses could be anything   windsurfers
Gliding toward the Dumbarton Bridge   or the old Fords
Lowered and leaded and polished   cruising
Toward Redding   or the heat   coming down
From Sacramento   heading south   on El Camino
As if California was still a dream
That might come true

                I can't see
        The tote board   but beneath the visor
    In the slanted shadow of the sun   I can see the names
    Turbulator Silver Mallet   Red Wind   Berset's Shadow
    And once   Quiet Little Table
    Who ran at Aqueduct and Bowie   Longacres
    Playfair   finally falling   on the dusty backstretch
    Of a county fair   whose name I can't remember

               But I remember orchards

Of roses   trembling flames   of leaves   and fields
Bright and long as the years   where the only horses
Still alive pull rakes   plows and harrows
Through the thick grass of someone's idea of beauty   and logs
Down the skid roads of the Siskiyous   buggies
Through the golden streets of Sutter's Mill   and silver
Nets across the salt coast of Big Sur

                    Until   the thick clouds   rising
From the cold waters of East Bay   become houses
I can build and live in   ships   I can sail
Through oceans of moonlight   horses
I can name   and ride

EXHIBITION PARK

From here in the cool shade
Of the grandstand the horses glide
Under the thin color of clouds, their breath mingling
With the pink and green and yellow silks toward the starting gate,
As smoothly as the swing of tails and braided manes, each horse led
By the scarlet coat of a groom. Their sleek bellies, fragile
Brush-stroked legs, the soft sway of light
Enter the gates, and the fog of colors
Washes over us, until they rise from the stalls
With the power of dust, like sunlight
Through water, like our rising hopes.
                              And I want
The photo to finish now, caught in the flash
Of blurred faces or the water-color
That has stained the wall in my den for fifteen years
Or the ocean beyond where the tide is forever
Coming in, finished before the finish
Line, before the winner's circle becomes a ring
We can't enter, when we might have won,
While the roses are still wet bursts of blood
Shimmering somewhere at the bright edges
Of the crowd.

CLOSING PORTLAND MEADOWS

Half-way across the Columbia River
Bridge, heading south, the eighth pole is a splinter
Of driftwood, the charmed circle of the grandstand
A sodden ship going down in the wreckage of a swamp
For the third time
I can remember. The parking lot is empty
But for two garbage trucks and the cleanup
Crew sitting on plastic bags, with last week's programs in their hip pockets
Like extra wallets, sorting discarded tickets, still looking
For a winner.
    For there were cold, December
Days, and flags snapping under the threat of rain and snow and strikes
And ash coming down from St. Helens. The track was small and dark
  and hard
On everyone, but there were sprinters straining in the gates, and five
Furlong long shots, and "bug boys" three pounds under, and the quiet
Hours studying The Form. For $5 you could get down
A Quinella, for $2 The Double, or simply $6 across the board
On the gray horse in any four horse
Field.
    But now, with nothing to bet on
But the wind tossing its voice
All the way from Reno, the marvelous, mortal world
Where betting on living flesh
Is something next
To possibility, like our childhood
Belief in angels
Who trusted the flashing air to hold them
Up and it did,
Is gone.

THE SIDE OF THE ROAD

If I could I would begin
Again, with the shallow stream that found its way
Beneath the wide street that still runs
Half the length of California and past the wonder of the vacant lots
And wildflowers to disappear into the silence of the weeds at the edge
Of the backstretch of Bay Meadows Race Track.
                              I would begin with the train
Ride to San Francisco, that dead hour
Between thought and motion, the tracks that rose
From the sea as salt, and smoke that stained the dark
Wall of the city.
                       I'd start by walking
To the exact spot where a three-year old filly fell
Through the fog on both broken legs, and the boy who woke
To the cold mud of the infield
Feeling nothing of this world
But his own pain.
                       I'd start with the wasted
Hours I burn each night, and the miles
That drive endlessly West, trying to become as wise as the child
Whose name I answer to.
                              Tonight,
While on the radio Jagger sings about horses, and the years that bend
Like those battered guardrails at the side of the road, and my son coughs
In his sleep, I'll climb
The one steep hill in San Mateo and look down
On the huge, white clouds
Breaking the tired back of August and smile
For all the hands that hold on and the shining
Wings of breath
That know better.

ARTIFICIAL HEART

I don't know how it can work   but it does
Measuring the strong flow
Of blood   the pulse loud and steady as it is
Clattering like the broken tongue
Of a bell that sings   live   live
Windmill of white wings still beating   angel with an actor's face
Rich tool   new valentine
On a short cord   as if a lantern had shattered
Under the snow   but instead of drowning
In the weeping darkness had bloomed
And spread
                    Still   it holds together
What it can and I think   it no more ruins   the mystery
Of the center of love   than the landings have changed
The pastures of the moon   the myths
Of the cold orange face   the backdoor
To heaven   for what is lost
Is not love   but the weak fluttering   of muscles
The collapsing shell of veins   valves that are no more
Than valves   for the planets   still smile
Old fashioned and certain as the canals of Mars   or the white fire
It pours   from mouth to mouth   like any good magician
Whose sleeves hold silver
Coins   spinning rings of light   rainbow scarves   who can balance
Twelve plates at once   turn water into wine   make life
Out of the materials   at hand

THE THIN MAN

Myrna Loy.
It always been Myrna Loy. As Nora Charles, heiress,
As lovely as the black, silk gown
She's wearing, standing,
One hand on her hip, ordering five martinis
To get even
With Nick, laughing, waiting for someone
To offer her a cigarette, wanting
The mystery to be solved so the serious
Drinking can begin.
                At the dinner party the search
For the murderer seems an afterthought. She doesn't care
About the bruise
Of the crime, now covered, hidden
Like a flask of gin in the folds
Of a trench coat or the clothes
That were too big
For the thin man or that Asta, the wirehaired
Terrier, jumps from the sofa
As if it's his movie; he did find the body.
                And after subduing the culprit,
Who can blame William Powell,
In his best imitation of Dashiell Hammett, smiling
At her with adoration
That has little to do
With acting.
(And maybe, like Cary Grant,
In Topper, I can do something good,
Something that will last, with the ghost
I am becoming.)

BEING THE POEM

"Be . . . Be . . . Be the ball."

—*Caddyshack*

Bought a hand-made red, hipster hat at Goorin Brothers,
On the Ave, wore galoshes on the sunniest days,
Found a pogo stick at a yard sale, hopped
With the kangaroos at the zoo, wouldn't order
Off the menu unless it rhymed, caressed Christina's
Breasts as we rolled across the meadow,
Spoke in couplets until she left
Me, wrote with my toes
On a 1926 Olivetti typewriter, standing
In the rain in Havana, smoked Gauloises
Wrapped in newsprint. (I googled
tercet, terza rima, villanelle, sestina even
pantoum, so I'll know what to do
when it happens). I worked construction, boxed
A little, pretended I was a woman
From Boston, (wore short skirts
And pearls), drove a Mercedes convertible
Through the wet streets of Detroit, drank Pernod
Straight, chased it with Jack
On the rocks. Grew a beard, walked with a limp,
Carried Walt Whitman in my tweeds, presented myself
To the poets in Iowa, had lunch
Alone, then returned home,
Found a gutter and slept. Dreamed
Of sharpened pencils, paper
Neatly stacked, a six pack at hand, waiting
For that final burst of creation. Being a poem
Isn't easy.

THE STATE OF THE ART SONNET

> "Don't murder me."
>
> —*The Grateful Dead*

In the old days there was emotion behind cracked
Kneecaps, splintered ribs and teeth; the short swing of a baseball
Bat, a burning coat hanger or a long-distance phone call—
When a transmitter was attached
To the guy's jewels—meant rage! But today, where guns
Are cute as dildos, the contemporary hit-man,
Worried about retirement plans, IRAs and
Money, uses an Italian .22, soft nosed slugs,
Looks for some place beneath the muscle
At the back of the head. He shoots once.
The fuck is that? The bullet never shatters bone,
Never scares nobody, or takes them shaking out of bed.
Might as well hire a lawyer, forget about women or drugs or loans.
Nobody even notices, but one guy, and he's dead.

ANOTHER SOFT SHOE FOR SPRING

Behind doors
That have been nailed shut
For years they begin to wake, rising
From the half-opened trunks,
Trailing dust and faded scarves, with the ghosts of applause
In their trembling hands, snapping
The crumpled brims of shapeless hats, tapping canes
On the barely remembered floors, relearning
All the old steps.

They are stepping out
In rubber boots, in golf shoes, in slippers
That fit like their wrinkled second skins.
From side doors of cheap hotels they are gathering
Like the slow moving weather drifting lightly above them, carrying
Platters of hundred-year-old eggs,
    dragging what's left of their lives
Into the airy streets. Out of doors whose clasps have sprung
Leaks, over transoms, they are flowing out like music
Sung in all the wrong keys. Out of the silvery shadows
Of glass doors, now broken down, they are breaking out.

And their shadows are crawling
Up cellar stairs, up the slippery
Slides of coal chutes, out of the empty mouths of packing crates,
As slow as the sun. They are waiting in the wings
For some tattered curtain to rise, stepping up
To the dim footlights, with the only prop
That still works, the old red cut-out
Of the heart.

IN THE BADLANDS

> "What are you rebelling against, Johnny?"
> "Whatdaya got?"
>
> —*The Wild One*

Seattle. The hottest summer in memory. Nearly
A year and still going bad. Could the heat draining the light
From the dark sides of the leaves
Be a poem? Or Mike's call from Austin
Last night when he said if he let a year go
By without a call he'd be dead. Is that a poem?
The old man circling my desk stops to sit beside me,
Tips back his greasy baseball cap, grins a toothless grin, winks
At me, then spits in his hands and swings
An imaginary bat, ready to hit
Somebody.
    Motes
Of dust gather, break apart. Maybe something will come
From the titles I made last winter when I was so full of myself
And hope: but the lights are still frozen
Blue haloes in "Night Skiing", and the drowning man is still half-erased
By darkness in "The Swimmer", and the poets are gathered
But say nothing in "Finding My Voice".
     Maybe
The poem is in Sturgis, South Dakota
On the back of a chopped Harley with the hundreds
Of bikers we passed on the way back from New Haven, in black
T-shirts and leather, dirty Levis, sure The Badlands
Were named for them. Sure.

What I need to do is throw my leg over a flaming teardrop
Tank, kick it in gear, let the wind carve whatever
Tattoos it wants, let distance
Write the road. Wherever
It goes. Maybe nothing should be
Forced or thought out, just the winding trail
Of dawn rising, and the blood flying,
Free.

OLD FRIENDS

Though the sun has been lost for days and nothing rises
To stand beside you, but the yellow smoke from the alley and the first few
Stragglers stumbling through the vacant lots, to lead you where you must go,
Neither right nor left, but in a weaving line down the weaving street, and the
Old country of the block goes on one staggering step at a time, the day
Broken into short breaths that almost forgot you, and the torn faces
You can hardly remember, you keep going.
                                        You see the waves of regret
Disappear, the heavy sheets of sadness fall away, and the promises
From the other side of the world gather 'round, like old friends
Come again, out of the taverns and bars, to greet you and the path
Toward morning, shaken loose like the drunken song spilling once more
From your wet and trembling lips.

SAYING GOODBYE TO THE GRADUATES

It is because they can leave and remain
Innocent in what we remember that tonight we gather
Our coats and keys and begin
The slow walk to our car, perhaps touching
Hands, smiling but saying nothing as we drive
Slowly, carefully through the small town
They have grown up in.
               Later, remembering
That night, we might say it wasn't dark
Until well after midnight, perhaps some trick
Of the eye, some fragment of moonlight left on the porch
Like a leaf of flame no one else could see. We might imagine
A playground that holds the running sounds of our children, their faces
Floating through the still air, the quiet hiss of bicycle tires
In the damp grass.
             With morning
There could be tendrils of light as if it was the beginning
Of summer after their first year
Of school, or months later in the middle of March,
And cold climbing the thin fingers of ivy, we might not sleep
Well, but wake to snow crossing the half-opened
Skylight and think of the years to come, the childhood we live
And relive, recalling how easily darkness falls
And falls, how we continually invent our lives, and how
In the darkness there is time to create
Everything until it is perfect.

IN A CLASSROOM AT NIGHT

Look. The children are sitting still
In the darkness, barely breathing. Their faces
Are turned toward us. Waiting. What we have said
Washes over them like water.
Now they are growing stiff wings and rising
Through all the rooms we have built for them.

Note how their luminous eyes float
Away from us toward the flat sky. They are all we have
Ever hoped for and they are slipping away.

See how we sink like the ruined boats
We have made from our words? Remember
How silence kept them afloat? How they motioned
To each other in a language we had long since forgotten?

                                        They are moving
But we can no longer see them. Now we are drowning.
Not even the light from the other side
Of the water can save us.

THE DREAMS OF GERARD DE NERVAL

"... and when, one day, he was found in Palais-Royal,
leading a lobster at the end of a ribbon (because, he said,
it does not bark, and knows the secrets of the sea),
the visionary had simply lost control of his visions,
and had to be sent to Dr. Blanche's asylum at Montmartre."

—*Arthur Symons*

It is always morning. The fields of Europe begin to dissolve.
Everywhere Paris is dark and wet. The cafes are closed against the rain,
And the heavy wooden shutters begin to break open. Late March began
In the sea, and I must find what it was. In the bright caves on the ocean
Floor, with ribbons shining like water, pouring from my hands. There
Are so many things to know.

There are strange cities falling all around me. The bars are filling
With Arabs and English. Old women sell fruit and cigars in the streets.
I keep looking for the girl I love. But no one knows who I am.
A man, who says I must come with him, leads me away. All afternoon

Roaches grow on the thick, gray walls, and from the barred windows
I look at the sea, at the people of Normandie, who carry silk
Handkerchiefs, and walk, whole crowds of them, into the cell to drown.

ENCHANTMENT

Even now, an old woman herself, she still relives
That hour after she pushed the witch
Into the oven, how he cried as she held him,
Gently, as if he were her child,
His life saved by a cauldron
Of fire that freed and caged
Her forever in that stunning moment,
The dream turning
On the axis of a star.

ALL I HAVE

It may not be much, but today it's all
I have. The weathered sky, the Cascades
Swinging closer through the swirl
Of trees, the old man at the edge
Of the park, wearing three shirts, two coats
And a smile stained with dirt and tobacco. He's leaning
Against the peeling red bark of a Madrona, his back turned
To the rising, half-built condos.
                              His ear-flapped hat fits him
Like a boy out of the thirties, and I can imagine him
Shadow boxing down a dirt road, slipping
Punches under leaves prickled with light, his depression
Nothing new.
                 He's talking
Out loud, of sculls and the fine chop
On the water, a sliding cedar seat and bladed oars, the radiance
Of phosphorescence, the rippled circles fish leave
When feeding—When he was a boy . . . When he was
A boy. He bends to scratch a chart in the dust, a map
Tracing the tracks of electric trolleys, the names of towns
That no longer exist, as if it could help, as if each day could be made
To last forever.
                    He didn't die.
He still sorts through the dog-eared pages of his past—snow
Falling down night's cold back, photographs of sheep,
Hayricks, the sagging roofs of barns, letters waiting
To be sent—as if it were a book he'd written
And anyone who cared to could find the worn path
And climb it, pluck a story from the buckled shelf
Of his life, find a place beside him
And read.

CALLAN

Callan Smith was the best looking kid in school. He had straight black hair, wore a black suede jacket and played football with the same abandon he exhibited when he drove, drank or danced with the most beautiful girl I'd ever seen. He was a senior when I was a sophomore and for some reason, maybe simply because we lived near each other, would give me a ride to school in his '32 Ford which had a small block Chevy engine, red and white tuck and roll interior and was the baddest car in town. He gave me my first beer, first cigarette and one wet winter night rolled the car down an embankment. My left leg was caught beneath the car and I couldn't move. Callan had been thrown and some part of the frame had crushed him. He was sitting upright against the sheared trunk of a tree, his arms limp, his right leg twisted beneath him. One of the headlights was still on and the light bounced up off the ground in front of him. His face seemed to be swollen twice its normal size, blood oozed out of his mouth and nose but I swear he was looking straight at me and he tried to smile and then was gone. He visits me a couple of times a month, late at night, when I think I'm sleeping. He usually doesn't say anything but occasionally tells me we should go on a road trip, toss the empties out the window, find a new town where every girl is wild and willing. I sometimes think the nightmares will end someday but I know that's just wishful thinking. I've thought about why I can't forget that night. I think it's because I was helpless to do anything to help him. I could only look at him until the cops came, put a blanket over him and used a jack to free me.

SONG

He didn't die easily, but after nine years of fighting his throat was a fire he couldn't put out, and the songs he sang drifted away as cleanly and easily as the first time I remember hearing them falling down around me with the snow that spun like white fire, like the dream of Christmas, like magic.

It was 1945 or '46, I was four or five years old that first Christmas in my grandparents' house that even now rises in my memory as a palace of polished oak and cut glass that held an ice box filled three times a week by a god disguised as a man, in a leather apron who carried huge, brilliant blue blocks of ice hanging from a pair of dull tongs as if they weighed nothing at all. My brother and I would run from the maze of the basement, up the wide stairs through the dining room and living room, the dens to the second floor bedrooms, and across my grandfather's work room which sprawled through most of the third floor, then up the narrow, steep stairs to the wondrous attic that held round-backed metal trunks, stacks of magazines and books, wicker baskets bulging with coils of rope and wire, blueprints, mysterious things. And a dressmaker's dummy, boxes of discarded clothes, a worn bicycle, ice skates hanging from nails in the wall, wooden skis, the endless accumulation of thirty-five years.

That December the house sparkled with green boughs, and silver and gold tinsel; the crystal chandelier suspended in the front hall was a blaze of spinning light, and the dining room table shimmered with slices of steaming turkey, and glazed hams, bowls of golden gravy and small white china cups of olives and sliced carrots and wet, green celery. There were plates stacked with frosted cookies and wide boats of sweet, red cranberry sauce. In the middle of the table stood a regiment of delicate long stemmed goblets surrounding a heavy lead glass punch bowl that was always filled with rich, creamy eggnog for the guests who seemed to never stop arriving. The Christmas tree filled half the living room like a multi-colored tower of dreams.

My brother and I ate in the kitchen but could hear the laughter and the toasts and glimpse the adults every time the swinging doors opened to allow the platters to be carried back and forth in a supply line of riches. After eating a little turkey and mashed potatoes and no steamed carrots at all, and too much cranberry sauce, we were treated to plum pudding and mincemeat pie then taken to bed praying the morning and Christmas would arrive as soon as we closed out eyes.

I was nearly asleep when my father picked me up, put me in my robe and swung me to his shoulder and walked me out to the upper porch overlooking the entrance to the house. Snow was falling thick and white on the upturned faces of everyone who had now left the house and was singing carols. My father's voice was strong and full of laughter and the warm smell of brandy. I remember my mother calling from the yard, "Put him to bed, Frank, put him to bed. He'll catch cold." But she was smiling as she said it. He put me down and raised the glass first to my lips then his own, then turned and looked down. "Here's to you, Kate, and to all the children we'll have." The brandy only touched my lips, but the taste made me dizzy and filled my nose with a sweet, pungency that I can taste even now. Then my father carried me back to bed where I fell immediately asleep.

All that happened a long time ago, before cancer burned a hole in his throat. The last time he called I could barely hear him. He whispered that we'd get together in the spring and find a cold mountain stream to fly fish. I knew it was a lie when he said it. Two days later he shot himself. I don't blame him. There's no one to blame. At the funeral, for a moment, I called back that Christmas, his song rich and deep as memory.

LAST WORDS

The clouds
Are wayward kites,
Trailing strings of starlight and smoke
Next to the blossoming pear tree, its petals
On the cool glass of the windows
Like a child's whispered secrets before the storm
Of stars cleared the August night.
      The past smiling at me again, asking, how long
Can I wait, here, in the dust of sunlight, where apples ripen
In wooden baskets, and a carnival spins, 1956, tossing
Dimes in dishes, throwing three balls for a quarter, and kissing
The twins in the back seat of a '35 Ford.
      Fruit bats at sunset, the colors of pebbles
Polished by the sea of another century, swallows' nests
In the clay walls above the Naches River
Where I found crawdads, periwinkles, dragon-fly larva, bait
For the rainbows that rose from the deep bed
Of the past.
      Those times,
Before morning when we're still adrift
In dreams that replay who we were, what
Will become of us. Hours that I didn't think
Were important. But they are now.
      I've had everything
I could ask for and still do, from one voice or another.
So many pages written, but that's not all, that's not
Even close. I've still got some stories
Left, some lines as slow and inevitable as the last breath,
Last word.

WHAT WE LOVE

No rain today. And that's good
For the boats heading out
For halibut, silvers. It's good for the green shadows
Of leaves that fell some time ago, still hanging
Across the white scar of the day, draped
Behind what we love to call
Memory, those stories we never tire of
Telling.
        And it's good for the two boys, holding
An army blanket for cover, crawling through the tall grass
Along the edge of the river, past the red winged blackbirds
Nesting in the cattails, wanting to see cougar, wolf, elk, perhaps
A girl rising from the cool, green water.
        All that calls me
Back, tells me what I thought
I'd forgotten. The days of exploration, days
Of discovery moving toward me, returning
Like the taste of pan fried trout and the times
We lay awake all night under the bright
Cloud of stars.
        And the ongoing landscape, those
Trails. Who made them? Not us,
Although we like to think we did, following
A sunken road, searching for faces
As blurred as the fog they bring us, as surely
As the boys lying
In wait, brave as the hours to come, when we'll move
Through the trees like the shadows
We've become, accepting everything
The newborn world can give.

ANOTHER CHANCE

Steady as the heart's pulse, the sea
Colored with blood and oil, the tapping
Inside steel hulls, a Morse Code from the dead.
The sacred flames from an alder wood fire, the scaffolding
Washed away. So much
Is gone. The wings of the world
Carrying a storm of loss, no more
Smoke from the deserted factories, the torn sleeve
Of a woman's dress. God knows
I've not tried hard enough, but I will,
I will. Just give me another
Chance. I might get it
Right this time. At dawn bats escape
The light, entering an afterlife I can only imagine,
Carrying the darkness
With them so I don't have to.

CLOSING THE ROXY THEATER

> "The goddam movies. They can ruin you."
>
> —*J.D. Salinger*

I should probably stop living
In the past but warm Saturday afternoons
Like this one lift me up and I'm sitting in the balcony,
In the best seat in the house, leaning forward, my chin
On the rail, my brother, my cousin and I, riding
With the black and white shadows
Of Hoot Gibson, Bob Steele, Johnny
Mack Brown, herding little dogies on the lone prairie,
Chasing yellow-bellied cowards through the wilderness
Of the West, galloping down the dusty streets
Of Deadwood, Tombstone,
Towns where we belly up
To the bar, toss back shots of red eye, tip
Our ten gallon hats to the beautiful, blonde school
Marm, who blushes and looks away. I rode shotgun
For Wells Fargo, beat Wild Bill
At faro, faced Wyatt and The Kid
And lived to tell the tale.
                    I was as happy
As those Saturday Matinees,
When the news of the world was crowed by a rooster,
When there were double features, three cartoons,
And a serial, when the war was over, and we felt the future
Would be as easy as Flash saving Dale
From the evil clutches of Ming the Merciless,

Or Dick Tracy cornering Cueball in that rat infested
Sewer, snatching Tess Trueheart from his cruel arms,
At least until next week.
                    Then the trolley,
Just a block away on 1st Avenue, took me
Home.

THE TICKET OUT

Late, long before the rain stopped, before moonlight
Washed the river clean, there she was
Again, right on time, the Old Mother of Nightmares
Dragging the past like a tattered shawl, through the double shots
Of neon Jim Beam, staggering
Up to me, mouthing my name, taking me
Home with her, saying, Honey, it's going to be
All right. Really it is. Like the women
I hardly knew, passed out
Beside me, too late, too tired
To wait for me to come back, knowing the day
Is as long or short as we make it.
       For December is cold
Stones and ice. December is wind. December
Is brass tacks. And January is a death
Dream, a heavy sea deepening
With each wave, the ice cave's
Cleansing breath. That's all
I wanted. To rise from the ditch
Of memory, to board the train
Running on wheels of iron and rust, the weeds
Waving beneath me like bits of broken glass,
Fat tubers, fat thumbs, broken bones
On a string. The bloody stain of steel wool, bristles
Of the bogeyman. Last goodbyes. The ticket
Out.

REVIVAL

Sometimes I can't recall what I did
Yesterday, but I remember walking out
Of the theater, under the ringmaster's
Misdirection, few cars at the curb, fewer thoughts
Of anything
                            but Sophia's smile
That bloomed into a smirk, then laughter as she pushed
Them back and left them wanting
More, something to build
On, to dream through the sweat hot nights.
                      And later
Marcello rubbing sleep
From his eyes, seeing the marble dolphins
Crumbling around him, the fountains filling
With tears as if he cried for the coming loneliness
And the streets that lead
Backward like the heart's road,
Looped in memory, those love
Roads, coursing with blood, how far back I can't
Recall.
            They must be gone now, deep
Into the well of what mattered.
            But the road also goes forward
And can't be stopped any more
Than those small, black birds clouding the sky,
Or the heaven I looked up to, seeing stars
Both skyward and in the adoration of those faces
Before the lights went up, before the curtain
Of age fell over me, over the pale screen I left
Behind.

We were beautiful, crossing
The leaf strewn lawns, timeless, vivid as the wine
We drank, the red taste on our tongues
That never really goes away.
            I wish
It was easy and maybe it could be. I could turn on
The magic lantern, watch the others
Turn toward me, walk into the disappearing,
Knowing we are not
Lost in that shimmering glow but better
Than we were and will be
Again.

GRACE

"Tomorrow when I wake or think I do, what shall I say of today?"

—*Samuel Beckett*

That every morning the same two crows, at least I think
They're the same, stare
At me from the deck railing, their heads
Tilting this way and that, eyes considering me, waiting
To be fed. That the woman, dressed in a blue and gray
Uniform topped by an absurd summer
Pith helmet, strides
Toward me, bringing the mail. And a boy,
Standing on a wooden box, slides the red rubber mouth
Of a squeegee across the windows
Of the Thai restaurant.
              Cones from the Sitka Spruce spray
Seeds along the walkway, thistle and ragweed, Aso's old Miata
Leaking oil. A cloud of yellow jackets clustered
Above the air vents of Ala Mode Bakery. The sheen of the street
From last night's rain, and in the damp grass a depression,
As if someone or something slept there.
              Opening day,
As light and tenuous as prayer.

WALKING WOODLAND PARK

Sparrows cling to the limbs of the pine trees, trails awash
With snow ring the merry-go-round. Something is crawling
Through the mounds of leaves, a possum, possibly
A raccoon. I think I hear laughter from behind the slides
But I can't see a thing. It's well
After midnight and only street lights
Glow in the softness of fog. I can taste
Spices in the wind, the scents of cinnamon,
Wind fall pears. I sit with my back
Against the totem pole, try to imagine who
Cut those wings so I could fly
Again, at least for a while,
Before I have to walk home,
Knowing it will all end
Soon, but not
Quite yet.

ABOUT THE AUTHOR

Thomas Brush's poems have appeared in *Poetry, Poetry Northwest, Prairie Schooner, Iowa Review, Crazyhorse, North American Review, Shenandoah,* and many other journals and anthologies. He has been awarded fellowships from the National Endowment for the Arts, the National Endowment for the Humanities, the Washington Artist Trust, and the Washington State Arts Commission. His most recent published collection, *Last Night,* was winner of the Blue Lynx Prize. He lives in Seattle, Washington.